The Lion Queens of India

JAN REYNOLDS

Lee & Low Books Inc.
New York

My name is Rashila, and I love lions.

Lions are the symbol of my country, India. In my culture, lions represent courage, power, and strength. We like to think of ourselves as strong and courageous, just like our lions.

The lions in India are called Asiatic lions and stand a little smaller than African lions. Our lions have a loose fold of skin under their bellies and their weight can range from 240 to 420 pounds (109 to 191 kilograms). My favorite lions are the males that look brave and powerful as they gracefully prowl the savannah.

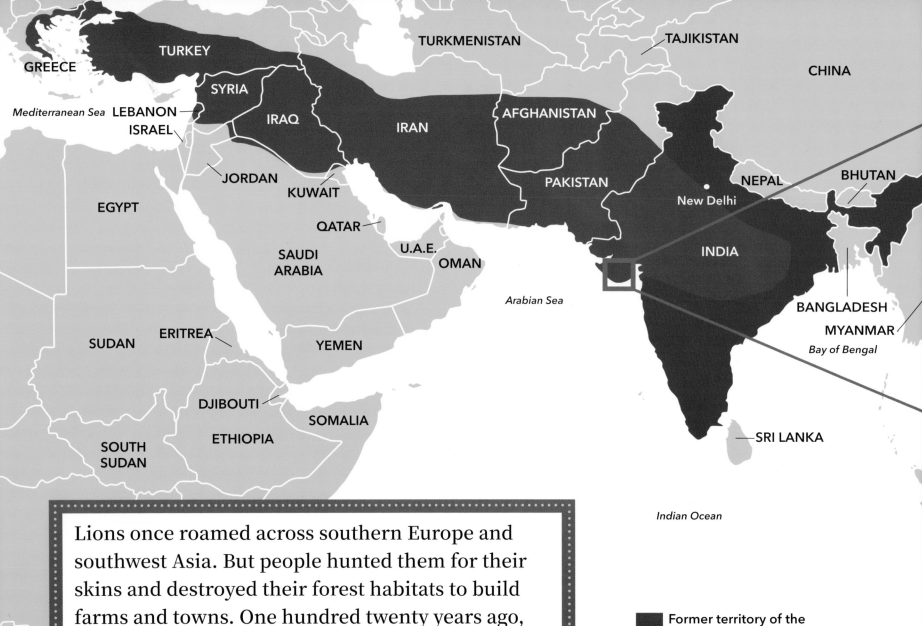

GREECE

TURKEY

TURKMENISTAN

TAJIKISTAN

CHINA

SYRIA

Mediterranean Sea LEBANON

ISRAEL

IRAQ

IRAN

AFGHANISTAN

JORDAN

KUWAIT

QATAR

U.A.E.

OMAN

PAKISTAN

New Delhi

NEPAL

BHUTAN

INDIA

BANGLADESH

MYANMAR

Bay of Bengal

EGYPT

SAUDI
ARABIA

Arabian Sea

SUDAN

ERITREA

YEMEN

DJIBOUTI

SOMALIA

SRI LANKA

SOUTH
SUDAN

ETHIOPIA

Indian Ocean

Lions once roamed across southern Europe and
southwest Asia. But people hunted them for their
skins and destroyed their forest habitats to build
farms and towns. One hundred twenty years ago,
the Asiatic lion almost became extinct. Only about
twenty remained alive.

Former territory of the
Asiatic lion

GIR NATIONAL PARK

GIR SANCTUARY

Arabian Sea

Then the Gir Forest in western India was made into a sanctuary, where animals could not be harmed or killed. Now more than five hundred lions live in this corner of India. There are no other wild Asiatic lions anywhere else on Earth.

When I was twenty-one, my brother wanted to become a forest ranger in Gir. He decided not to take the physical test, so I tried out instead. I passed and became the first female forest guard, and the other guards called me the Lion Queen.

Now there are many Lion Queens. We work with the other rangers to track and protect the lions. We also help maintain the natural balance of the forest and teach the neighboring villagers how to live peacefully with all the animals in the sanctuary.

Every day, I patrol a section of the forest on my motorbike, searching for lions. If I don't see them, I watch for their tracks on the ground. I use paw prints to figure out when lions last passed by this area. We track poachers this way as well.

We are trained to use guns to protect the lions, but my stick is often the only tool I carry. I pound it on the ground and call, "Hut-hut, hut-hut!" Some lions have known these sounds since they were cubs, so they are not threatened when I approach.

These concrete troughs make small drinking ponds for the lions. The forest can become dry in the summer months, so windmills pump water for the animals to share.

I often find the lions in the shade during the heat of midday.

A group of two to six lionesses and their cubs is known as a pride. Prides live and hunt together in a territory of about 19 square miles (50 square kilometers) in size. Two or three adult males form a group called a coalition that travels the same territory as a pride. Cubs begin to hunt after one year and are independent around three years. Then the male cubs leave their pride and eventually form their own coalition. Female cubs often stay with their original pride for life.

I know certain lions very well because their territory lies in the section of forest I patrol. Some are shy, some are playful, and some are more aggressive.

The lions may recognize us as rangers, but they are still wild creatures that follow their animal instincts. We always respect the lions and keep a safe distance.

When a ranger sees that one of our precious lions is hurt, we perform a `rescue`. I have been trained as an expert with a tranquilizing gun, which I use to put the lion in a short, deep sleep. Veterinarians can then treat the lion's wounds and keep it safe.

Sometimes a lion falls into an empty, abandoned water well. Then I must go down in a cage to tranquilize the big cat so we can lift it out. In my twelve years of service as a ranger, I have rescued more than a thousand animals.

Lions are **carnivores**, which means they eat meat. They use their strong jaws, fearsome teeth, and sharp claws to take down animals for food or defend their territory. Their claws also help them climb trees or fight other lions when needed.

Lionesses do the hunting to feed their prides, while adult males largely hunt for themselves. Most hunting happens just before dawn, when it is cool and quiet in the forest, or in the late afternoon around dusk.

The lions hunt creatures like the nilgai, above, and this spotted deer. Although I love my lions, I care about all of the creatures in Gir.

The Gir sanctuary environment is home to many kinds of plants and animals living in a natural balance called the **web of life**.

If one element of the web goes missing, then everything else can be thrown out of balance.

4 . . . and their droppings and other remains nourish the soil in turn.

1 The sun, water, and soil create conditions for plants to thrive.

3 These creatures then feed on one another . . .

2 The plants nurture insects, birds, fish, and animals.

Gir's web has been interrupted in the past.

In the early twentieth century, humans had hunted Asiatic lions to near extinction, and livestock had overgrazed and degraded the forest. Then greater protection was given to the lions and the forest. After the livestock population was controlled, the natural balance between the plants and animals returned. Soon the number of lions began to increase thanks to more wild prey and the protection by the forest guards.

We are happy about the growing lion population, but now we need more forest area for young male lions to find territories of their own. Yet the Gir sanctuary is surrounded by farms and villages, and people need land, water, and food just like lions do.

The question is, how can humans and animals both thrive, living near each other and competing for the same resources?

To address this question, we Lion Queens work with the **communities** surrounding Gir to teach them about the lions' needs and behavior. Visitors to the sanctuary can take vehicle safaris to learn about the lions' habitats and their role in the web of life we share.

These efforts help everyone understand the importance of living peacefully with all animals, including the lions.

We also hope to move some prides and coalitions to another area in India. If other forests can host lions, there will be more territory for the population to increase. Another sanctuary will also protect the Asiatic lion against a forest fire or sickness that could wipe out the population in Gir.

Another solution: more **Lion Queens**! We believe women make good rangers because the lion population has grown faster with female rangers working in the sanctuary. The Lion Queens are relaxed and confident around lions, and we work well with villagers.

With more education, more forest sanctuaries, and more Lion Queens, I believe we will save the Asiatic lion from extinction. If we save our lovely lions, the brave and powerful symbol of our Indian people, it will be like saving ourselves.

When we can save any wild species, we sustain the entire beautiful web of life on our planet, which in turn supports us all.

AUTHOR'S NOTE

I first met Rashila Vadher in her house, where she wore a colorful, traditional Indian sari—a floor-length cloth wrapped over a short blouse. She told me she was very busy, but if she could get permission and time, she would take me into the Gir sanctuary to track some lions. I had traveled to India in hopes of meeting some of the Lion Queens, but I never dreamed I would meet Rashila herself—the very first woman to become a "Forest Guard," or ranger, in Gir.

A couple days later, I hopped on a motorcycle behind Rashila, now dressed in her uniform, and we took off on the dusty trail into the forest. She taught me about the Gir sanctuary, the monsoon cycle, how to track lions, and all the animals of the sanctuary: crocodiles, peacocks, leopards, monkeys, and so much more. The Gir sanctuary is a dry, deciduous forest, 545 square miles (1412 square kilometers) in size, with no set physical boundaries—it is simply surrounded by local farms and villages. The Gir forest became a reserve in 1913 to save the last remaining Asiatic lions. In 1965, it became a wildlife sanctuary, and in 1975, the central part of the sanctuary was declared a national park. The sanctuary is now full of rich biological diversity, including thirty-eight species of mammals, thirty-seven species of reptiles, more than three hundred species of birds, and more than two thousand species of insects. I was struck by Rashila's knowledge of the diverse wildlife and depended on her to keep me safe while we moved through the sanctuary.

I could see that Rashila loved her job and was very humble about how well she performed her work. She was quick to tell me she succeeded at being accepted as the first female Forest Guard because the veterinarian at the animal hospital saw her determination and skill and decided to train her as a tranquilizing expert. The male Forest Guards then called Rashila whenever an animal was injured or in trouble, and she gained their respect with her accuracy and calm. Rashila told me the support of this veterinarian made a big difference in her life, because before that point, as a woman, she had continually been asked to take a desk job.

Rashila has had a one hundred percent success rate with her rescues, which number more than a thousand, and she has become the head of the rescue department for the Gujarat Forest Department, which includes the Gir sanctuary. Because of her success, more women have become Lion Queens, and they are pleased their work is helping the lion population increase.

Jan Reynolds and Rashila Vadher

Still, as Rashila made clear to me during my visit to Gir, more education of the local people and more space for the lions themselves will be necessary to maintain a healthy population of Asiatic lions. Moving beyond Gir, the story of the Asiatic lion teaches us the need to protect not only endangered species but all species of plants and animals in order for Earth to thrive. If you can support the preservation of the wild lands and natural parks in your area, and advocate for creating more, you'll support all the great diversity of life on our amazing planet, including these wonderful Asiatic lions.

—Jan Reynolds

ACKNOWLEDGMENTS

My primary sources for this book came from my fieldwork in the Gir sanctuary in January 2018 and interviews and ongoing conversations with the following people in the Gujarat Forest Department: Rashila Vadher, three-star ranger and Head of Rescue for the Department; Darshana Kagada, two-star forester; Dinesh Sadiya, certified guide and photographer; Nalin Ramoliya, computer operator and photographer; and Ramadan Nala, director of the Wildlife Division. Ashish Kmr Rout served as my translator when necessary, and Mary A. Callahan provided technical support in the United States. My trip was funded in part by the Bay Paul Foundation, the James Robison Foundation, and the Oakland Foundation. I also appreciated the expertise of Dr. Ravi Chellam, CEO, Metastring Foundation, Bengaluru, Karnataka. Any remaining errors are my own.

Darshana Kagada

BIBLIOGRAPHY

Hardikar, Jaideep. "Infectious Outbreaks Threaten the Last Asiatic Lions." *Scientific American*, December 10, 2018. https://www.scientificamerican.com/article/infectious-outbreaks-threaten-the-last-asiatic-lions/.

International Union for Conservation of Nature/Species Survival Commission Cat Specialist Group. "Asiatic Lion." Accessed June 7, 2019. http://www.catsg.org/m/index.php?id=113.

Lipton, Gabrielle. "Into the Lion's Den in Gujarat." *DestinAsian*, December 2015/January 2016.

Principal Chief Conservator & Head of the Forest Force, Government of Gujarat. "Gir National Park and Wildlife Sanctuary." Accessed June 7, 2019. https://forests.gujarat.gov.in/gir-nat-park.htm.

Seetharaman, G. "What's Stopping the Asiatic Lions of Gir from Getting a New Home?" *India Times*, October 20, 2018. https://economictimes.indiatimes.com/news/politics-and-nation/whats-stopping-the-asiatic-lions-of-gir-from-getting-a-new-home/articleshow/66296056.cms.

United Nations. "UN Report: Nature's Dangerous Decline 'Unprecedented'; Species Extinction Rates 'Accelerating.'" UN Sustainable Development Goals. May 6, 2019. https://www.un.org/sustainabledevelopment/blog/2019/05/nature-decline-unprecedented-report.

Zoological Society of London. "Protecting Asiatic Lions in the Gir Forest." Accessed June 7, 2019. https://www.zsl.org/conservation/regions/asia/protecting-asiatic-lions-in-the-gir-forest.

This book was made with love and respect for Rashila Vadher, Darshana Kagada, Dinesh Sadiya, and Nalin Ramoliya. May your efforts save the Asiatic lion from extinction. —J.R.

Photo credits: 2: courtesy Rashila Vadher / Gujarat Forest Department • 3: clockwise from top left: Nitin Kelvalkar / Dinodia; Nitin Kelvalkar / Dinodia; Christophe Boisvieux / Dinodia; CSP_mkistryn / Dinodia • 4: Nalin Ramoliya • 5: Nalin Ramoliya • 6: underlying map by dikobraziy / shutterstock.com • 7: Gir map created by Eric Gaba and used under a CC BY-SA license via Wikimedia Commons, customized for this book by Charice Silverman; lion: Nalin Ramoliya • 8: left: Jan Reynolds; right: courtesy Rashila Vadher / Gujarat Forest Department • 9: Anindito Mukherjee / Reuters • 10–13: all photos: Jan Reynolds • 14: Nalin Ramoliya • 15: Dinesh Sadiya • 16–17: courtesy Rashila Vadher / Gujarat Forest Department • 18: lioness: Nalin Ramoliya; lion: Dinesh Sadiya • 19: nilgai: Anindito Mukherjee; spotted deer: Jan Reynolds • 20–21: background image, peacock, and deer: Jan Reynolds; Crimson Rose butterfly: Charles J. Sharp, used under a CC BY-SA 4.0 license via https://commons.wikimedia.org/wiki/File:Crimson_Rose_(Pachliopta_hector)_underside.jpg; rohu: Yasir Shahzad / Shutterstock; black-naped hare: Milan Zygmunt / Shutterstock; lion: Nalin Ramoliya; seedling: Sushobhan Badhai on Unsplash • 22–23: all photos: Jan Reynolds • 24: top, Anindito Mukherjee / Reuters; bottom: Jan Reynolds • 25: Nalin Ramoliya • 26: Nalin Ramoliya • 27: Anindito Mukherjee / Reuters • 28: Jan Reynolds • 29: Nalin Ramoliya • 30: courtesy of Jan Reynolds • 31: top, Jan Reynolds; bottom, Dinesh Sadiya • 32: Nalin Ramoliya

Text and selected photos copyright © 2020 by Jan Reynolds
All other photographs copyright © by their respective photographers, used with permission

LEE & LOW BOOKS Inc., 95 Madison Avenue, New York, NY 10016
leeandlow.com

Edited by Cheryl Klein

Book design by Charice Silverman

Book production by The Kids at Our House

The text is set in Noto Serif and Flamenco

Printed in Malaysia
10 9 8 7 6 5 4 3 2 1
First Edition

MIX
Paper from responsible sources
FSC® C144853

Library of Congress Cataloging-in-Publication Data

Names: Reynolds, Jan, 1956- author.
Title: The lion queens of India / by Jan Reynolds.
Description: First edition. | New York : Lee & Low Books, 2020. | Includes bibliographical references. | Audience: Ages 6-8 | Audience: Grades 2-3 | Summary: "An introduction to the Asiatic lion and the 'lion queens,' or female forest rangers, of the Gir wildlife sanctuary in Gujarat, India"— Provided by publisher.
Identifiers: LCCN 2019043181 | ISBN 9781643790510 (hardcover)
Subjects: LCSH: Vadher, Rashila—Juvenile literature. | Forest rangers—Women—India—Biography—Juvenile literature. | Lions—Conservation—India—Juvenile literature.
Classification: LCC SD129.V33 R49 2020 | DDC 599.7570954—dc23
LC record available at https://lccn.loc.gov/2019043181